The Essential

MERCEDES-BENZ
W123
All models 1976 to 1986

Your marque expert:
Julian Parish

VELOCE PUBLISHING
THE PUBLISHER OF FINE AUTOMOTIVE BOOKS

www.veloce.co.uk

First published in March 2018 by Veloce Publishing Limited, Veloce House, Parkway Farm Business Park, Middle Farm Way,
Poundbury, Dorchester, Dorset, DT1 3AR, England.
Fax 01305 250479/e-mail info@veloce.co.uk/web www.veloce.co.uk or www.velocebooks.com.
ISBN: 978-1-845849-26-9 UPC: 6-36847-04926-3

British Library Cataloguing in Publication Data – A catalogue record for this book is available from the British Library.
Typesetting, design and page make-up all by Veloce Publishing Ltd on Apple Mac.
Printed and bound in India by Replika Press.

Introduction
– the purpose of this book

"The finest saloon car of the 20th century," "The Mercedes that defined a generation" …

The W123 series has established a reputation for the ultimate quality in Mercedes-Benz' long history. Built at a time when the design of its cars was led by engineers, not by accountants or marketers, Mercedes aimed to produce the best possible vehicle in its class, regardless of cost. More than 40 years have passed, however, since the W123 was launched in January 1976, time enough for any car to show its weaknesses. This guide will help you identify potential trouble spots and choose among the extensive range of models offered.

Development work on the W123 started in 1968, just as its predecessor, the so-called 'Stroke Eight' series, was introduced, with the aim of providing greater safety, improved comfort and better serviceability. Thanks to innovative features such as the new double wishbone front suspension based on that used in the W116 S-Class, an anti-dive braking system and improved energy absorption in accidents, the W123 combined up-to-date technology with proven engineering.

Its styling was noticeably more modern than the previous W114/W115 range, helped by a switch from vertical to horizontal headlamps, as with the W116 S-Class and R107 SL models. Seen today as a classic, it stands out from the later W124 and W201 models with its generous chrome trim and traditional details like its painted hubcaps.

Like its predecessor, the W123 was sold as a standard saloon (sedan), a long-wheelbase saloon, and a coupé, the latter two models introduced in 1977. For the first time, however, Mercedes also offered an estate (wagon) as a regular production

Coupé, saloon and estate seen together. (Courtesy Mercedes-Benz Classic)

model, with production starting at its Bremen plant in April 1978. No fewer than 17 different engines were available during the W123's ten-year career, including four- and six-cylinder petrol engines and four- and five-cylinder diesels. Despite relatively high prices, the range was a huge success right from its launch, with waiting lists of up to three years for the coupés.

At first, the W123 may seem to appeal to the head more than the heart, and a basic saloon now appears quite austere. With their pillarless construction, however, the coupés are among the most elegant two-door models that Mercedes ever built. The estates, too, have become very popular as stylish-yet-practical classics which can be used every day, and they now command the highest prices of any W123 models.

Offset head-on collision test shows improved accident safety. (Courtesy Mercedes-Benz Classic)

Lack of central pillar characteristic of Mercedes' coupés. (Courtesy Mercedes-Benz Classic)

Thanks

The W123 series has a large number of enthusiastic supporters, and I am grateful to many of them for their help in preparing this guide, especially Martyn Marrocco from the UK Mercedes-Benz Club, Leigh Holbrook of ToWiW123, and Rory Lumsdon and Rachel Goodwin at Mercedes-Benz UK. Silvie Kiefer at Mercedes-Benz Classic in Stuttgart was most helpful in providing the archive pictures used in the book.

Once again, my thanks are also due to the great team at Veloce Publishing, and in particular Rod Grainger and Lizzie Bennett.

Contents

The Essential Buyer's Guide™ currency
At the time of publication a BG unit of currency "⬤" equals approximately
£1.00/US$1.34/Euro 1.13. Please adjust to suit current exchange rates.

1 Is it the right car for you?
– marriage guidance

Tall and short drivers
All drivers should be comfortable behind the wheel. The lower roofline of the coupé means less headroom for tall drivers, although lowered seat mountings were available as an option.

Weight of controls
Power-assisted steering was initially fitted as standard only on the 280, 280E and 300D models, and, without it, the car will feel heavy and ponderous to drive. The long travel of the accelerator pedal may make the car seem sluggish.

Will it fit the garage?

Model	Length	Width	Height
Saloon (sedan)	186.0in/4725mm	70.3in/1786mm	56.6in/1438mm
Coupé	182.7in/4640mm	70.3in/1786mm	54.9in/1395mm
Estate (wagon)	186.0in/4725mm	70.3in/1786mm	57.9in/1470mm
Long-wheelbase saloon	210.8in/5355mm	70.3in/1786mm	58.3in/1480mm

Interior space
The saloon and estate both offer comfortable space for five passengers. The coupé was built on a wheelbase 8.5cm (3.3in) shorter than the saloon, and is best suited to two in the back. The estate was available with an optional rearward-facing folding seat in the luggage compartment, which can carry two children – or you could always look for a long-wheelbase (LWB) saloon, with room for eight!

Luggage capacity
The saloon and coupé models both have room for at least 500 litre (18ft³), but the rear seat backrest is fixed, so there is no scope for carrying longer loads. There are no such worries with the estate models, with a luggage capacity of 879 litre (31ft³) to the window line with the seats folded down, leaving a long, fully carpeted load bay. A split-folding rear seat was available as an option, and all estates were originally fitted with a double roller blind, covering the luggage behind the seats, and protecting rear seat occupants from items flying forward.

Usability
These cars' durability and practicality make them an ideal choice for the owner new to classic cars, or for daily use.

Parts availability
Availability of mechanical parts – some of them interchangeable with other Mercedes models – is generally very good, whether from Mercedes-Benz itself, independent specialists, or through the worldwide network of Mercedes clubs. Body and trim parts, however, can be more problematic, particularly for the coupé and limousine. Mercedes-Benz has let some parts go out of stock, and there are fewer good cars left to plunder for parts. Interior trim, especially in velour, or in less popular colours, can prove harder to find.

Roomy front seats.
(Courtesy Mercedes-Benz Classic)

Spacious luggage
compartment on saloon.
(Courtesy Mercedes-Benz Classic)

Parts cost

Most routine service parts and mechanical components are reasonably priced.
Some chrome trim, such as the horseshoe-shaped piece on the side window of the
coupé (●x800), can be frighteningly expensive. Some parts which have gone out of
stock are now being remanufactured, but at much higher prices than before.

Insurance

Most insurers will cover the W123 under classic car policies, sometimes with
mileage limitations or alongside a modern 'daily driver.'

Investment potential

Prices of both the coupé and estate models (especially the six-cylinder 280CE/
280TE and the 300TD versions) have risen markedly of late, with scope to move up
further. Values of the saloons are more stable, with only modest increases likely.

Foibles

The W123 car is a rational car with few
idiosyncrasies. On cars with manual transmission,
the foot-operated parking brake can take some
getting used to.

Plus points

- Conservative, classic styling
- Expensive feel and prestige of Mercedes brand
- Outstanding build quality

Minus points

- Limited performance of diesel-engined cars
(except 300 Turbodiesel)
- Lack of sporting appeal (except 280E)

Alternatives

Audi 100, BMW 5-Series, Ford Granada,
Volvo 240/260.

Elegant, pillarless
lines, but less room in
the coupé. (Courtesy
Mercedes-Benz Classic)

2 Cost considerations
– affordable, or a money pit?

Purchase price
Basic four-cylinder petrol and diesel saloons are the cheapest way into W123 ownership, with cars in good running order starting well under ●x5000. ●x10,000 should get you a well cared-for 230E or 250 saloon (sedan) with moderate mileage. The coupés – especially in six-cylinder form – are considerably more expensive, commanding up to ●x20,000 for a car in excellent condition. The estates (wagons) have often been worked hard, making it increasingly difficult to find low-mileage cars in good condition. As a result, the top 280TE and 300TD models can fetch over ●x25,000.

Servicing
Looking after a W123 is relatively straightforward, with oil and filter changes recommended every 6000 miles and a full service due every 12,000 miles.
• Brake fluid: change every year
• Coolant: change every three years
• Sparkplugs: change every 12,000 miles
• Fuel filter: change every 24,000 miles
   The W123 makes little use of electronics, and with fewer electric 'goodies' as standard (even the window winders were manual as standard), there is less to go wrong. It can be easily maintained without complex test equipment or special tools.

Parts prices
Prices shown are for OEM parts from Mercedes-Benz and for a final-generation 230E saloon from 1983, unless otherwise shown. Cheaper alternatives may be available, but check their quality.

280CE awaiting service.

Mechanical parts
Air filter ●x20
Fuel filter ●x40
Sparkplugs (set of 4) ●x15
Radiator ●x130 (independent)
Head gasket ●x25
Water pump ●x240
Timing chain kit ●x250
Exhaust manifold ●x400
Exhaust (complete) ●x590
Wheel bearing ●x80
Front anti-roll bar ●x300
Front shock absorber ●x190
Rear spring ●x100
Pressure accumulator for self-levelling
rear suspension (estate) ●x530
Steering damper ●x30
Steering idler ●x65
Tyre (175 SR 14) ●x60 (independent)
Front brake pads ●x50
Front brake disc (each) ●x45
Brake master cylinder ●x240
Battery ●x100
Central locking vacuum pump ●x90

Body parts
Bonnet (hood) ●x1100
Underbonnet insulation pad ●x45
(independent)
Front wing ●x300
Front apron ●x25
Rear quarter panel ●x570
Front bumper ●x500
Rear bumper ●x610
Front door ●x400 (independent)
Door seal ●x50 (independent)
Windscreen ●x440
Windscreen seal ●x80
Alloy wheel (Fuchs) ●x140
(independent)
Painted hubcap ●x210
Halogen headlamp ●x215
(independent)
Tail light assembly ●x350
Set of overmats ●x120 (independent)

Replacement underbonnet
insulation pad.

This chrome bumper section is ready to
be replaced.

Body-colour hubcap with
chrome embellisher.

www.velocebooks.com / www.veloce.co.uk
Details of all current books • New book news • Special offers • Gift vouchers • Forum

9

3 Living with a W123

– will you get along together?

Good points

For many enthusiasts, the W123 series epitomises all they like most about Mercedes' postwar cars. Elegant without being flashy, the conservative lines of the W123 are set off by the extensive use of chrome trim. Later Mercedes models would turn to plastic trim mouldings, and for many enthusiasts the W123 represents the last and best in a long line of traditionally styled, mid-sized cars from Stuttgart. The bold paint colour options (red, orange, yellow, and even avocado green) and matching trim also mark the W123 as a car of the Seventies, although more subdued or traditional colours including white, silver and dark blue were offered too.

Driver's airbag optional from April 1982. (Courtesy Mercedes-Benz Classic)

Underneath its conservative body, however, the W123's engineering was exemplary, combining well-tried features with major innovations, in areas such as suspension design, braking and safety. Mercedes continued to improve the car during its career, with a new generation of four-cylinder petrol engines (designated M102) introduced in 1980.

Features such as the reinforced passenger cell and door beams and the collapsible steering column make the W123 one of the safest cars of its era. With automatic (inertia-reel) seatbelts fitted all round, and the later options of ABS and a driver's airbag, the W123 should reassure partners or family members worried about travelling in an older car.

Each model in the range has its own appeal. The saloon (sedan) may seem plain to look at, but it is a great all-rounder, with space for five passengers and their luggage, and a comfortable ride. Details such as the characteristic ribbed tail lights (designed to keep them clean in bad weather), will delight the connoisseur.

Inviting saloon rear seat, here with velour trim. (Courtesy Mercedes-Benz Classic)

The estate (wagon) is surely the most sensible version of all, with its generous luggage space and self-levelling rear suspension to compensate for heavy loads, whilst retaining the superb finish of the saloon and coupé models. The optional rear-facing folding seat makes it an ideal choice for classic car enthusiasts with a large family, as it is one of the few classics with room for seven.

The coupés, on the other hand, are certainly not lacking in style. With the sunroof open (a frequently fitted option) and all four side windows wound down with no central pillar to intrude, they are wonderful cars to enjoy by the coast or on a country backroad in the summer.

Spacious and well-trimmed estate. (Courtesy Mercedes-Benz Classic)

Thanks to their reliability and exceptional build quality, all the W123 cars can still be driven on a regular basis, even every day. With the exception of the lower-powered diesels (200D, 220D and 240D), all the cars have enough performance to keep pace comfortably with modern traffic.

Bad points

For some would-be buyers, the W123 range – at least the saloons and estates – will simply appear too sensible, and lacking in that element of fun which they consider essential in a car to be driven at weekends and on holidays.

Models fitted with the higher-revving fuel-injected 2.8-litre engine (280E/280CE/280TE) have a decent turn of speed, and, in its day, the 280E achieved some memorable rallying successes, notably on the 1977 London-Sydney Marathon and the 1978 East Africa Rally. The other petrol-engined models, however, are best suited for gentler cruising, and should not be considered in any way sporting. The four- and five-cylinder diesel models will probably be too slow altogether for many would-be owners in today's traffic; the 200D offered just 55bhp in what is, after all, a relatively large and heavy car.

Whichever model you are looking at, the handling is certainly surefooted, but the huge steering wheel and large number of turns lock-to-lock can make the car feel unwieldy.

Coupé photographed in winter in the Tyrol. (Courtesy Mercedes-Benz Classic)

There is a huge variety of models to choose from, but your first decision will probably be the easiest: is it to be a saloon/sedan, coupé or estate/wagon? How each car drives is then largely dependent on the engine fitted, with a wide choice from 55bhp four-cylinder diesel to 185bhp six-cylinder petrol. You may also want to consider the differences between model years and any special equipment fitted, but for a car of this age, its originality and overall condition will probably be more important.

Estate, saloon and coupé on Mercedes' test track. (Courtesy Mercedes-Benz Classic)

Which body style?
Of the 2.7 million W123 cars built, 88% were the standard-wheelbase saloons, so you will have plenty of choice. Initially, most saloons had two round headlamps on each side, and the broad rectangular headlamps were fitted only to the 280/280E, but, from September 1982, these were standardised across all models.

The long-wheelbase saloon (or V123) is a specialised choice, and only 13,700 vehicles were built. It was available in 240D, 300D and 250 (petrol) versions and was used mainly by hotels and as a taxi. Nicknamed 'The beanpole,' its wheelbase was extended from 2.80m (110in) to 3.43m (135in), allowing space for a folding third row of seats and an optional glass divider behind the driver. Self-levelling rear suspension, uprated brakes and 15in wheels were fitted. The LWB chassis also served as the basis for special-bodied ambulances and hearses.

Nearly 100,000 C123 coupés were produced, mainly in four-cylinder 230C/CE and six-cylinder 280 C/CE form. In the US, however, to meet the CAFE (Corporate Average Fuel Economy) requirements, the coupé was also sold with a five-cylinder diesel engine, from 1977-81 as the 300CD, and from 1981-85 as the 300CD Turbodiesel. In Europe, all coupés had the broad rectangular headlamps fitted to the 280/280E saloon and, until 1982, chrome air inlet grilles under the windscreen. The coupé was considerably more expensive than the equivalent saloon, but came with extra equipment, including power steering and lower-profile tyres. Mercedes did not offer a factory-built convertible, but some independent coachbuilders developed their own expensive conversions, such as Crayford's St Tropez.

In the past, Mercedes-based estates had been built by specialists such as Binz or Universal, but, with the S123, the manufacturer offered its first factory-built estate. The letter 'T' was added to each model name, designating 'Tourism & Transport.' These cars are now much in demand, especially in good condition and with moderate mileage. The self-levelling rear suspension makes them ideally suited for carrying heavy loads and for towing.

Extra length of LWB saloon is clear here. (Courtesy Mercedes-Benz Classic)

Which engine?

Many buyers today will opt for a petrol engine: although economical and smooth for their time, the naturally aspirated diesels are slow (even the 300D develops only 80bhp). They face increasing restrictions on their use in urban areas, due to their high emissions. The diesels, especially the 300D and the 300 Turbodiesel estate (in continental Europe – it was never offered in RHD form for the UK), still have their fans though, thanks to their mechanical simplicity and incredible longevity, many covering more than half a million miles.

US-spec 300CD coupé. (Courtesy Mercedes-Benz Classic)

At launch, the W123 carried over the M115 four-cylinder engines from the 'Stroke Eight' in 200 and 230 guise, but a new single-cam 2.5-litre 'six' (the M123), producing 129bhp, was

Period advertisement for Crayford's St Tropez convertible.

fitted exclusively in the W123. In 1980, the M115 units were replaced by the much more modern and efficient M102 engines, again in 2.0- and 2.3-litre form. Fitted with fuel-injection, the 230E, which produced 136bhp, proved highly popular and makes an excellent all-round choice today. At the top of the range, the M110 in the

M123 engine unique to the W123 250.

M110 twin-cam engine
from the 280/280E.
(Courtesy Mercedes-Benz Classic)

280E is a superb twin-cam in-line 'six,' with a much sportier power delivery; until 1981, it was also offered in carburettor form.

Manual or automatic?
The manual gearchange (with four or five speeds, depending on the model) can be heavy and notchy. Hill starts can be awkward, especially with the foot-operated parking brake fitted to left-hand drive cars (right-hand drive cars have a pull-out parking brake release on the dashboard). As so often with Mercedes, most W123s are best enjoyed with the manufacturer's excellent four-speed automatic transmission, leaving the manual gearbox to the lower-powered diesels, where the automatic saps even more of their power.

Traditional stepped gate
for automatic transmission
selector.

Which generation?
Over its ten-year life, the W123 went through two major face-lifts. In September 1979, the changes were most obvious inside, with smaller head restraints, a new design of steering wheel and a herringbone weave to the cloth seat trim, replacing the original check pattern. In September 1982, the second face-lift brought improved levels of equipment, with power steering, the broad rectangular headlamps and a wooden trim strip on the dashboard now standard on all cars. The final cars also received better rust protection.

First-generation saloon with check
pattern cloth trim.

5 Before you view
– be well informed

To avoid a wasted journey, and the disappointment of finding that the car does not match your expectations, it will help if you're very clear about what questions you want to ask before you pick up the telephone. Some of these points might appear basic, but when you're excited about the prospect of buying your dream classic, it's amazing how some of the most obvious things slip the mind ... You can also check the current values of the model which attracts you in classic car magazines, which give both a price guide and auction results.

Where is the car?
Is it going to be worth travelling to the next county/state, or even across a border? A locally advertised car, although it may not sound very interesting, can add to your knowledge for very little effort, so make a visit – it might even be in better condition than expected.

Dealer or private sale
Establish early on if the car is being sold by its owner or by a trader. A private owner should have all the history, so don't be afraid to ask detailed questions. A dealer may have more limited knowledge of a car's history, but should have some documentation. A dealer may offer a warranty/guarantee (ask for a printed copy) and finance.

Cost of collection and delivery
A dealer may well be used to quoting for delivery by car transporter. A private owner may agree to meet you halfway, but only agree to this after you have seen the car at the vendor's address to validate the documents. Alternatively, you could meet halfway and agree the sale, but insist on meeting at the vendor's address for the handover.

View – when and where
It is always preferable to view at the vendor's home or business premises. In the case of a private sale, the car's documentation should tally with the vendor's name and address. Arrange to view only in daylight, and avoid a wet day. Most cars look better in poor light, or when wet.

Reason for sale
Do make it one of the first questions. Why is the car being sold, and how long has it been with the current owner? How many previous owners?

Imports
The W123 is one of the most popular classic cars in Germany, with plenty on sale. Some German-market cars, especially from the lower end of the W123 range, however, have a very basic specification.

When you buy a car from another country, you may need to make changes to the number (licence) plates, lighting (headlamps and indicators) and radio equipment. If you re-register a car from Germany or another EU country within the

EU, you may need to obtain an attestation from Mercedes-Benz that it conforms to the original specification.

For buyers in the UK and other countries which drive on the left, you may find some cars which were originally assembled in South Africa and which have a specific ADB prefix for their Vehicle Identification Number (VIN): these are generally considered very well built, but had only minimal underbody wax protection, increasing the risk of corrosion in damper climates.

Condition (body/chassis/interior/mechanicals)
Query the car's condition in as specific terms as possible – preferably citing the checklist items described in Chapter 9.

All original specification
An original equipment car is invariably of higher value than a customised version.

Matching data/legal ownership
Do VIN/chassis, engine numbers and licence plate match the official registration document? Is the owner's name and address recorded in the official registration documents?

For those countries that require an annual test of roadworthiness, does the car have a document showing it complies (an MoT certificate in the UK, which can be verified on 0300 123 9000 or www.gov.uk/check-mot-status)?

If a smog/emissions certificate is mandatory, does the car have one?

If required, does the car carry a current road fund licence/licence plate tag?

Does the vendor own the car outright? Money might be owed to a finance company or bank: the car could even be stolen. Several organisations will supply the data on ownership, based on the car's licence plate number, for a fee. Such companies can often also tell you whether the car has been 'written-off' by an insurance company. In the UK, these organisations can supply vehicle data:

HPI – 0845 300 8905; www.hpi.co.uk/
AA – 0800 316 3564; www.theaa.com/
DVLA – 0300 790 6802; www.gov.uk/get-vehicle-information-from-dvla/
RAC – 0330 159 0364; www.rac.co.uk/

Other countries will have similar organisations.

Insurance
Check with your existing insurer before setting out: your current policy might not cover you to drive the car if you do purchase it.

How you can pay
A cheque/check will take several days to clear, and the seller may prefer to sell to a cash buyer. However, a banker's draft (a cheque issued by a bank) is as good as cash, but safer, so contact your own bank and become familiar with the formalities that are necessary to obtain one.

Buying at auction?
If the intention is to buy at auction, see Chapter 10 for further advice.

Professional vehicle check (mechanical examination)

There are often marque/model specialists who will undertake professional examination of a vehicle on your behalf. Owners clubs will be able to put you in touch with such specialists.

Other motoring organisations with vehicle inspectors that will carry out a general professional check in the UK are:

AA – 0800 056 8040; www.theaa.com/
RAC – 0330 159 0324; www.rac.co.uk/
Other countries will have similar organisations.

Exceptional 230TE, on sale at the Retro Classics show in Stuttgart.

www.velocebooks.com / www.veloce.co.uk
Details of all current books • New book news • Special offers • Gift vouchers • Forum

17

6 Inspection equipment
– these items will really help

This book
Reading glasses (if you need them for close work)
Torch
Magnet (not powerful, a fridge magnet is ideal)
Probe (a small screwdriver works very well)
Overalls
Mirror on a stick
Digital camera (or smartphone)
A friend, preferably a knowledgeable enthusiast

This book is designed to be your guide at every step, so take it along, and use the check boxes to help you assess each area of the car you're interested in. Don't be afraid to let the seller see you using it.

Take your reading glasses, if you need them to read documents and make close-up inspections.

A torch with fresh batteries will be useful for peering into the wheelarches and under the car.

A magnet will help you check if the car is full of filler. Use the magnet to sample bodywork areas all around the car, but be careful not to damage the paintwork. Expect to find a little filler here and there, but not whole panels.

A small screwdriver can be used – with care – as a probe, particularly in the wheelarches and on the underside. With this you should be able to check an area

of severe corrosion, but be careful – if it's really bad, the screwdriver might go right through the metal!

Be prepared to get dirty. Take along a pair of overalls, if you have them.

Fixing a mirror at an angle on the end of a stick may seem odd, but you'll probably need it to check the condition of the underside of the car. It will also help you to peer into some of the important crevices. You can also use it, together with the torch, along the underside of the sills and on the floor.

If you have a digital camera or smartphone, take it along so that, later, you can study some areas of the car more closely. Take a picture of any part of the car that causes you concern, and seek a friend's opinion. Like the mirror on a stick, a 'selfie stick' may help you get your smartphone under the car.

Ideally, have a friend or knowledgeable enthusiast accompany you: a second opinion is always valuable.

Raising the bonnet to the service position will let you inspect the engine more easily. (Courtesy Mercedes-Benz Classic)

A screwdriver will help you check for rust in places like this.

www.velocebooks.com / www.veloce.co.uk
Details of all current books • New book news • Special offers • Gift vouchers • Forum

19

7 Fifteen minute evaluation
– walk away or stay?

Its reliability and the quality of its engineering have helped make the W123 one of the most popular and sought-after modern classics. With nearly 2.7 million cars built, there are plenty of survivors, so take your time and choose carefully. Be ready to walk away if you find a major problem or the car simply doesn't feel right.

From long-distance rally champion to Moroccan taxi, the W123's toughness has never been in doubt. (Courtesy Mercedes-Benz Classic and iStock)

Exterior

Start by checking that the car sits level and square on the road. On estates and other cars with self-levelling rear suspension, make sure this is working with the engine running.

Condition of sills and jacking points is critical.

The rear wing and side window of this estate are in a sorry state.

Since all W123s are now at least 30 years old, some scratches are inevitable, unless the car has recently been restored. But dented panels, scuffed alloy wheels and badly worn tyres all suggest a car which has been poorly cared for. Look carefully along the line of the car on each side for dents or uneven panels, then step back to check for mismatched paint on different parts of the body, which may be the result of poor repairs.

The climate a car has lived in will have a huge effect on its condition. Cars from cold, wet areas – even more so where salt is used on the roads in winter – will be much more prone to corrosion than cars from warmer, sunnier climes. Rust is the W123's biggest enemy today. Look carefully at all parts of the car, especially below the waistline. Are the doors, wings and wheelarches solid? How do the sills and jacking points look? What about the panels below the front and rear bumpers? If you can look at the car from underneath, can you see signs of corrosion, on the rear subframe or exhaust system, for example?

Hot, sunny weather is not all good news, however. Over time, rubber trim and fittings tend to harden and perish. Take a look at the seals around the doors and

20

all the windows, especially the front and rear screens and, on the estate, the rearmost side windows. If these dry out, damp can get in, allowing rust to take hold.

The W123 has plenty of chrome: is all the trim present and in good condition, or have parts such as the bumpers begun to rust through? Is the traditional Mercedes three-pointed star damaged, or even missing altogether? On coupés, pay particular attention to the side window trim.

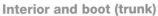

Are the chrome bumpers and other trim still looking good? (Courtesy Mercedes-Benz Classic)

As you walk around the car, check the age and condition of the tyres: a matching set of recent tyres from a premium brand, with plenty of tread remaining, is a good indication that the last owner has looked after the car well.

Many estates in particular were fitted with a tow bar. If this is the case, check whether the electrical connections are in good condition, and ask the seller if the car was used regularly to tow a caravan or other trailer, as the extra load may have put more strain on the transmission and brakes.

Interior and boot (trunk)

The interior of the W123 is exceptionally durable (especially on those cars with MB-Tex vinyl upholstery) and should still look good. Look for cracks in the dashboard top or other plastic trim, and for worn or faded upholstery. Check for signs of abnormal wear on the driver's seat side bolster, gearknob or steering wheel, especially if the recorded mileage is low. Do all the seats remain firm and supportive? Collapsed springs are a common problem on the driver's seat. Lift the carpets and check for signs of dampness resulting from water leaks. On cars with sunroofs, inspect the headlining for water stains.

With the ignition key turned to the accessory position, turn on the lights and see whether the dashboard lighting works as it should. When you start the engine – after waiting for the glow plugs on diesel-engined models – check that all the warning lights go out. Do all the lights, including those for the rear number plate, work correctly? There are relatively few electrical items to check on a W123, but make sure that any optional equipment (such as electric windows or sunroof) functions normally.

With the boot open, check that the standard emergency warning triangle is clipped to the underside of the lid. Lift up the carpet and the

Velour upholstery rarely stands the test of time as well as this. (Courtesy ToWiW123)

Check that all the instruments and warning lights operate normally.

Don't forget to take a close look inside the boot. (Courtesy Mercedes-Benz Classic)

spare wheel, and look into the recesses of the boot and the spare wheel well for any signs of corrosion. If the car is indoors or in poor light, use a torch for a better view.

The engine compartment

Release the bonnet from inside the car and pull on the tongue protruding from the radiator grille to open it. If you are not familiar with Mercedes' cars of this era, ask the seller to raise the bonnet to the fully upright service position, so that you can examine the engine more easily. This needn't be immaculately clean, but should be free from obvious leaks. If the car has been standing, look underneath for signs of oil or other fluid leaks. Are the different hoses and the sound insulation pad in good condition, or have they dried out and cracked? If you can get underneath the car, have a look at the various rubber bushings and gaiters on the suspension.

Pull on this tongue to open the bonnet. (Courtesy Mercedes-Benz Classic)

Bonnet fully opened. Note the missing sound insulation. (Courtesy Mercedes-Benz Classic)

No untoward leaks on the straight-six engine of this 280E.

Modifications

Is the car you are looking at in its original, standard specification, or have any aftermarket parts been fitted? If the performance has been increased, have the brakes and suspension been upgraded to match, using high-quality parts? Most collectors now prefer standard, unmodified cars.

Is it genuine and legal?

However attractive the car may look at first, it's essential that the paperwork is in order. First of all, does the car you are viewing match the description in the advertisement? You can confirm the model by looking at the VIN (the 17-digit

Vehicle Identification Number); the VIN plate or sticker on the car should, of course, tally with that on the registration/title document. Make sure that the VIN hasn't been tampered with, and take a note or photograph of it for reference. You can look it up online later to confirm the year of manufacture of the car or check its specification. Independent organisations (see Chapter 5) will also let you check that there is no finance outstanding on the car and no record of serious accident damage. If something doesn't seem right here, walk away now. At best, you may have problems registering the car; at worst, it may be stolen or unroadworthy.

Try to find out as much as you can about why the car is being sold. There are still some genuine W123s being sold by their original owners (or their families), perhaps after they have given up driving. Coupés were often bought as second cars for more occasional use. Often, cars such as these will have low mileages and comprehensive service records. Evidence of work carried out over the past few years is especially valuable, whether it covers regular maintenance or the replacement of major items such as the timing chain fitted to the M102 engine in the 200 and 230E from 1980. Don't be put off by stamps in the service book or invoices from independent specialists: they often have more expertise in working on cars of this generation than official Mercedes-Benz dealerships.

Sometimes, however, the reason for sale will be less encouraging. There may be a big repair job looming, or the seller may have run out of time or money to complete a restoration. Ask to see the latest MoT certificate (in the UK) or records of other safety inspections: did the car pass with flying colours, or is there a long list of advisories, which may be costly to put right? These may not be reason enough to reject the car, you may be able to negotiate a reduction in the price or ask the seller to include some spare parts in the deal.

Only buy a W123 from an individual who can prove that they are the person named in the car's registration document (V5C in the UK) and, preferably, at the address shown in the document. Also check that the VIN on the car matches the number in the registration document (see Chapter 11 for more details).

Cars originally supplied to the United States can be identified at once by their larger bumpers. (Courtesy Mercedes-Benz Classic)

Road test

If the seller refuses to take the car out or let you drive, be ready to turn away. A road test taking in a variety of city traffic, open roads and motorways (freeways) is essential to assessing any car. Before starting off, check that the insurance covers you to drive, and that the indicators, lights and wipers all work. Try and start the engine from cold if possible: it should start readily and idle smoothly. As soon as you give the engine some revs, the oil pressure gauge should move to its maximum reading. On cars with fuel-injection, try starting the engine when it is warm as well, for example at the end of your test drive.

Keep the radio off and listen out for any untoward noises. Uneven running can be a particular problem on the carburettor-equipped 250 and 280 models, but it may also be the result of valve damage. A loud knocking noise when accelerating may signal a damaged conrod or worn main bearings. Look out too for blue smoke from the exhaust, which may be the result of valve guide wear. Repairing this is particularly expensive on the 280 models. Excessive wind noise often occurs when the window seals have perished.

On a clear stretch of open road, take your hands off the steering wheel: the car should continue to run straight. If it doesn't, an alignment check may be required. Some free play in the steering (a maximum of two fingers) is considered normal, but more than this will mean that adjustment or an overhaul of the steering will be needed.

If the car you are testing is fitted with automatic transmission, forward and reverse drive should both engage cleanly, and all changes should be smooth, whether made automatically, using kickdown or the manual override. On cars fitted with manual transmission, make sure that the clutch engages and disengages smoothly without slipping. The gearchange is naturally notchy, but you should be able to select all gears without any untoward noises or obstruction.

When traffic conditions allow, apply the brakes hard: the car should pull up straight. Few W123s were equipped with anti-lock brakes (ABS), so watch out for the wheels locking up, especially in the wet. Any judder means that the discs (rotors) are warped or corroded and should be replaced. Try to test the parking brake on an incline, to ensure that it will hold the car securely.

Include some driving at higher speeds when you test the car.
(Courtesy Mercedes-Benz Classic)

8 Key points
– where to look for problems

Exterior
• Are all the panels straight, with even gaps?
• Is the colour and finish of the paint consistent?
• Are there signs of rust, especially on the wings, wheelarches and sills?
• Is all the chrome trim present and in good condition?
• Are all the seals for the doors and windows in good order?

Does it look as good now as when it was new? (Courtesy Mercedes-Benz Classic)

Interior
• Does the overall condition of the interior look consistent with the mileage shown?
• Is the upholstery (particularly cloth and velour) in good condition, or is it faded or worn?
• Do all the seats (especially the driver's) provide proper support?
• Are there any signs of damp under the carpets, or stains on the headlining?
• Do all the instruments and electrical equipment work correctly?

Are all the chrome fittings, such as the big bumpers and radiator grille, still in good condition? (Courtesy Mercedes-Benz Classic)

Engine and mechanicals
• How does the engine compartment look? Dirty and uncared for, or suspiciously clean?
• Are there any oil leaks or light-coloured stains where coolant has escaped?
• Are the different hoses secure and in good condition, or has the rubber perished?
• Does the car sit level? Pay particular attention to cars fitted with self-levelling rear suspension.
• Are the tyres recent and in good condition?
• Is there a service history showing regular maintenance and any major work carried out?

Velour trim is less common on the saloon. (Courtesy Mercedes-Benz Classic)

Unless the car has been restored, be wary of engine compartments with no signs of use. (Courtesy Mercedes-Benz Classic)

9 Serious evaluation
– 60 minutes for years of enjoyment

Score each section using the boxes as follows: 4 = excellent; 3 = good; 2 = average; 1 = poor. The totting-up procedure is detailed at the end of the chapter. Be realistic in your marking!

If you've come this far, well done! The paperwork is in order and the car looks promising. Now is the time to take a really thorough look over it, bearing in mind the points already mentioned in the last two chapters. Try and work your way systematically around the car, so that you don't miss any nagging details. Start outside with a close look at the bodywork, before turning your attention to the interior and, finally, the engine and underbody.

Exterior

First impressions · 4 · 3 · 2 · 1

Make sure that you can view the car outdoors and in daylight, preferably in good

Show quality? Not all W123s will look as good as this 280.

weather. The car should be clean; it's hard to judge the condition of paint under a layer of dirt or dust. Begin by stepping back from the car and noting how it sits on the road. Does the car appear to sag on either side or at one end? On estates (wagons) and long-wheelbase saloons fitted with the self-levelling rear suspension, check, with the engine running, that this system is operating correctly.

Do all the panels and trim line up perfectly, as on this estate? (Courtesy Mercedes-Benz Classic)

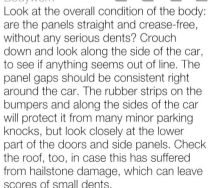

Bodywork · 4 · 3 · 2 · 1

Look at the overall condition of the body: are the panels straight and crease-free, without any serious dents? Crouch down and look along the side of the car, to see if anything seems out of line. The panel gaps should be consistent right around the car. The rubber strips on the bumpers and along the sides of the car will protect it from many minor parking knocks, but look closely at the lower part of the doors and side panels. Check the roof, too, in case this has suffered from hailstone damage, which can leave scores of small dents.

If the bumpers appear badly damaged, check for other signs of accident damage, such as uneven panel gaps. At the front, the chassis legs had small pleats to help absorb impacts: if these have closed up, you should check more closely for signs of a previous accident.

Paintwork defects marked up on the door of this coupé.

Paintwork

The paintwork should be consistent in colour and an even depth across all panels, which you can measure (in microns) with a thickness gauge. Differences in adjacent areas may suggest that an area has been poorly filled, or that a localised respray has been carried out. Look particularly around the rear wheel arches and below the car's waistline, and examine the flat upper panels (roof, bonnet (hood) and boot (trunk) lid, which may have been bleached by the sun in hot climates.

Body corrosion

If the section that follows seems alarmingly long, it should not be inferred that the W123 was especially vulnerable to corrosion. Indeed, in many ways these cars were better built than many contemporary models. The cars are so strong mechanically that these bodywork issues inevitably stand out all the more.

The earliest W123s are, however, more than 40 years old, and were built during a time of world steel shortages, leading to the use of some poorer-quality steel from Eastern Europe. German taxi drivers – who were important and demanding customers of the W123 – soon complained about the early onset of corrosion, and Mercedes responded by improving the quality of steel used and the five-stage zinc phosphate rust protection employed, particularly after 1981. Better cavity wax injection was applied, full-size plastic wing liners were fitted, and the water channels were redesigned to carry excess water away more effectively.

Even if a mud flap offers some protection, the rear wheelarch and the bottom of the wing are vulnerable.

Wings and wheelarches

The wings and wheelarches are among the W123's most common rust spots. The wings rust from the outside and may well have been replaced. Beware of cheap replacements, especially from the Far East; good-quality parts should show even panel gaps and well-finished leading edges. The fixing kit should have been renewed at the same time. Rust where the top of the wings meet the A-pillars is not unusual, but repairing it is labour-intensive, requiring up to 20 hours' work on each side.

Rust is already advanced on this wheelarch.

Rust on the wheelarches, in particular on earlier cars (plastic inner wing liners were fitted from 1978 onwards), is frequent. Beware of chrome wheelarch trims – more popular when the cars were new in North

America – as these can trap moisture and hide the onset of corrosion. Look inside the wheelarches, too, especially near the pick-up points for the rear axle and at the metalwork behind the headlights.

Chassis and sills

The condition of the sills is often indicative of a car's overall condition, and, on the W123, rust frequently lurks behind the chrome trim strips under the doors. Take a close look at the jacking points, which allow dirt to get in; soon, damp and rust will take hold. Plastic covers can be fitted to alleviate this problem, which can otherwise lead to the car failing a safety inspection. Some sills may have been poorly repaired with swathes of filler, which a small magnet will detect.

This jacking point and the sill coating should be treated to stop rust worsening.

Underneath the car, the rear subframes frequently suffer from corrosion. Although the complete assemblies – which are expensive to replace – can be restored, this is a major job. Well documented by the UK Mercedes-Benz Club and elsewhere, it is best undertaken by a professional. An examination of the rear chassis legs is especially important for cars used for towing, fitted with Mercedes' own tow bar, which bolts into these.

The front box-section chassis legs can also rust, if water is allowed to get into the front footwells, but this can be hard to see from underneath the car, so try to lift up the carpets and sound-deadening from inside the car, to inspect the floorpan from above. If you can get underneath the car, look for signs of rust around the front suspension mounts and the seatbelt anchorage points, a vital safety consideration.

Other areas

The bottoms of the doors rust, particularly on cars from the first year of production, which lacked the broad rubber strip and beading at their base. On saloons and estates, the holes where the wiring for the rear door runs through from the B pillar can rust, if the rubber grommet perishes or drops out, allowing water to get in.

The front apron and the panel in front of the windscreen can both rust, the latter especially, if the ventilation grilles become blocked and trap moisture. The bonnet rusts on its leading edge, often when stone chips are left unrepaired.

The front edge of this bonnet is already rusting badly.

Look down the side of the radiator for rust at its base.

Look for rust under the battery.

With the bonnet open, look down the radiator for signs of rust on the lower radiator mounting brackets. You may also find corrosion on the bonnet hinges and around the suspension top mounts. While you are there, take a look under the battery tray (powder-coated replacements are available), brake master cylinder and ABS pump (when fitted). Make sure that the drain holes are clear, to prevent rust spreading to the engine bulkhead. For cars fitted with the optional headlamp wipers, watch for water building up in the small moulded recesses where these are fitted.

Chrome and other trim

The W123's plentiful chrome trim is a key part of its appeal, but it needs to be in good condition to do justice to the car. The substantial front and rear bumpers can rust through, including where the rubber strip is fitted. They are expensive to replace, especially the three-section bumpers fitted to the coupés and 280/280E. Cars destined for the North American market had much more substantial impact-absorbing bumpers, to comply with local legislation.

All the chrome trim tends to go dull over time, but can usually be revived by polishing. The fine chrome strips on the radiator grille are vulnerable to small dents. Along the side of the car, the chrome trim strips are screwed on and can rust from underneath, so watch for any paint bubbling as a warning sign. Make sure that they are securely attached, to prevent dampness getting in and setting off further corrosion.

The horseshoe-shaped chrome trim around the rear side windows on the coupés is easily scratched and is especially costly to replace (●x800). On the estates, the condition of the chrome roof rails should be inspected. The original 280/280E saloons had additional chrome trim for the air inlet grilles under the windscreen and strips under the rear light, so this should also be examined.

US models such as this 1981 Turbodiesel saloon had extended bumpers. (Courtesy Mercedes-Benz Classic)

Impressive chrome 'horseshoe' trim on the coupé should be in good condition.

Check for corrosion around and underneath the ventilation grilles.

Wheels

All the cars were equipped with 14in wheels, except the long-wheelbase saloons and a few cars assembled in South Africa, which had 15in wheels.

If the painted hubcaps appear shabby, a special kit is available from Mercedes to repaint them;

Painted hub caps typical of Mercedes' cars of the 1960s and '70s.

Handsome Fuchs alloy wheels like these rarely suffer from corrosion.

the UK Mercedes-Benz Club's archive includes a helpful guide to doing this job. Using a sponge and warm water rather than a power washer will keep them looking good.

The optional Fuchs alloy wheels (sometimes known as 'Mexican hat' wheels on account of their design) are high-quality forged items and corrosion is rare.

Glass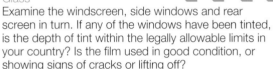

Examine the windscreen, side windows and rear screen in turn. If any of the windows have been tinted, is the depth of tint within the legally allowable limits in your country? Is the film used in good condition, or showing signs of cracks or lifting off?

The condition of the windscreen is especially important, as it is most likely to be damaged by stone chips. A crack in the driver's line of sight may cause the car to fail a roadworthiness inspection, such as the MoT test in the UK. A replacement windscreen could be used as a bargaining point, if the car looks good otherwise.

Examine the seals carefully on all the windows: inevitably, these will perish over time. The seals will then let in water, causing corrosion around the front and rear screens or inside the door panels. Carefully open the side windows: as the rubber seals on these

Badly rusted coupé door mirror fillets.

perish, the metal clips can scratch the glass as the windows are wound down. Some seals, such as those for the coupé rear side windows, are now being remanufactured. The rear-quarter window mechanisms are time-consuming to repair.

The small seals which hold the door mirror in place swell with age, and can prevent the window glass from lowering correctly. If the seals perish, they will let in damp and cause the metal fillet to rust.

Sunroof

Score four points if not fitted: one less thing to go wrong, and more headroom into the bargain!

When fitted, the sunroof was always electrically operated on the saloons (sedans) and coupés, but manually operated on the estates. Check that it opens and closes smoothly; the rails should be cleaned and greased annually.

Seen from inside, this sunroof panel is free from stains.

Above all, ensure that the drain holes are clear. With the seller's permission, pour some water down the holes and look for it running out under the sills. If these holes become blocked, you are likely to see traces of rust around the opening and telltale stains on the roof lining, especially behind the sunvisors. Repairs can be expensive, as it will be necessary to remove the entire headlining and the rear screen. If unchecked, blocked drain holes will lead to damp under the carpets, which will eventually cause the floor pans to rot. If you see signs of condensation in the car, investigate further.

Coupés

The doors fitted to the coupé are longer and heavier than on the other models in the range. If any damp has got inside them, due to perished door or window seals, more water can accumulate, increasing the extent of corrosion along their bottom edges. Gently prise away the door seal along the bottom and look for signs of rot.

The rear screen is also larger and is more prone to water getting in. Check for corrosion round its outer edges, which may suggest further rust behind the seal. Removing the screen to deal with this is a job best left to specialists.

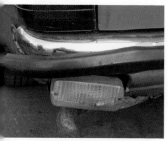

Damaged reversing light and rubber bumper strip on this 240TD.

Rust bubbling up under the side window trim strip: a common problem on estates.

Estates (wagons)

Despite their 'lifestyle' positioning, many estates were used hard, with heavy wear inside the luggage compartment common. The gas-filled tailgate struts can lose strength, especially in cold weather, so be sure to try lifting the tailgate a few times. Make sure, too, that the rear locking mechanism – which is complex and requires regular lubrication – works as it should, and that the rear windscreen wiper operates smoothly, as the driveshaft can corrode and seize up. The rear fog and reversing lights are very exposed to parking damage, and are often cracked or broken altogether. Take a quick look inside the fuel filler: the neck area picks up debris, and rusts, causing leaks.

The condition of the tailgate itself is important, as it is a stressed member of the bodywork. Check for rust at its base, often due to water leaks around the rear screen, causing water to seep inside and accumulate there, as there are no drain holes. Look, too, for rust around the main tail light assemblies and under the rearmost side windows: in the worst cases, water can get inside the luggage compartment.

If you are planning to use your car to tow, Mercedes' own tow bar (made by Oris) is much to be preferred, as it attaches to the chassis legs. Aftermarket parts bolted directly to the floor of the car can cause severe corrosion.

Interior

The outstanding build quality of the W123 should be apparent inside as much as outside, and it can be hard to guess the real mileage a car has covered. Some trim parts are no longer available new, so it is worth looking for a vehicle with a complete interior.

Look at the dashboard for cracks or tears along the top (blue trim is especially vulnerable to UV rays), and for damage caused by poorly installed audio equipment there (or from speakers on the rear parcel shelf). The rear shelf, together with the top of the rear seat, can also fade, if exposed to too much sunlight, while the wood trim strips may bleach or come unstuck.

Are the carpets still clean and in good condition? Replacement floor mats are no longer available from Mercedes, but high-quality alternatives (using the original patterns) are available from independent specialists such as Classic Mercedes Mats (classicmercedesmats.co.uk).

Remove any overmats which are fitted and lift the edge of the carpets to check for damp underneath. There are several possible causes for this, which will need to be investigated further: they include rust at the rear of the battery tray, perished rubber seals for the windscreen, or blocked sunroof drainage holes.

While you have all the doors open, take the chance to inspect the door seals carefully. Like the window rubbers, these can dry out over time and will let water into the car, fostering corrosion. They are expensive to replace (●x800 on the coupé) and require considerable skill to fit well.

Olive-green cloth interior, edged with vinyl. (Courtesy Mercedes-Benz Classic)

Missing wood trim on dashboard will need to be sourced.

Seats and upholstery

The seats in a Mercedes W123 should have a naturally springy feel: Mercedes used individual springs, like those on a bed, with uprated springs available for the 'larger driver.' Over time, the spring bases can fail, especially on the driver's seat, causing the seat bases to collapse, and making the car feel wallowy to drive, even when the suspension is in fact in perfect order. The only real solution is to replace the springs and rebuild the seats, a job best left to professionals.

Many saloons and estates were fitted with cloth upholstery (to the centre sections only, with vinyl edges, until the 1982 face-lift). These can wear at the edges, or rip, and are liable to staining. Mercedes' textured vinyl upholstery, known as MB-Tex, is legendary for its toughness. Leather upholstery was an expensive option, most commonly found on coupés. Velour upholstery was also available as

Unmarked beige leather, despite this car's 123,000 miles (198,000km).

Note the ribbed side sections on these brown velour seats. (Courtesy ToWiW123)

an option, with ribbed sections on the outer section providing improved grip. It is a wool-rich material, which is comfortable in cold weather, but prone to wear and fading.

Luggage compartment

Unmarked spare wheel well in freshly restored saloon bodyshell.

The spare wheel well is a natural water trap, and the seller should not object to your lifting the spare wheel to check for corrosion and confirm that the drain plugs underneath are clear. It pays to look carefully into the recesses of the boot using a torch. If you see any signs of damp or corrosion, this may have several possible causes (which are well explained in the UK Mercedes-Benz Club Forum), including leaks from the seals around the rear screen, boot lock or tail lights, or from a disconnected drain pipe inside the fuel filler recess.

Coupés

The luxurious appearance of the coupé interior is further enhanced by the walnut trim fitted to the dashboard and centre console on earlier models, rather than the simpler Zebrano-style wood which was standard on the saloons at the time. Check the condition of this: if it needs to be refurbished, it can be hard to match the grain and colour of the wood, and sometimes replacing the complete set of trim parts is the only solution.

The front seat backs should be held in place with a vacuum locking mechanism: check that this operates correctly with the engine running.

Estates

Make sure that the rear seat folds down correctly, and that the roller blind (which should be present on all 'T' models) works as it should. If the desirable folding third row of seats is fitted, ensure that this folds smoothly and that the seatbelts are in good order.

The rear screenwash reservoir can crack and is a further possible source of leaks inside the luggage area on this model.

Mesh blind in place in an estate.

Electrics and ancillaries

For many would-be purchasers, the W123's simplicity and lack of electronic gadgetry will be an essential part of its appeal, and there is certainly far less to go wrong than with later models. What electrical equipment is fitted is typically reliable, too.

Instruments and controls

The odometers regularly fail, and the cars' durability means that high mileages often go undetected. Look for tell-tale signs such as smooth patches on the steering wheel rim or gear knob, or excessive wear on the pedal rubbers, and check the mileage recorded on service documents or inspection certificates for any discrepancies. Incidentally, you will find many cars with a large clock on the right of the instrument panel and no rev counter; the latter only became standard on all petrol models in October 1980.

Make sure that the combination switch on the steering column (for the lights, wipers and indicators) works correctly. Each item of optional equipment (such as the electric windows or passenger door mirror, or the sunroof on saloons and coupés) should also be tested.

Does the mileage showing on the odometer seem plausible?

Do any optional extras work as they should? These switches on the centre console are for the passenger door mirror and heated front seats.

Original Becker Europa radio with manual tuning.

Audio systems

In-car entertainment was a much simpler affair in the W123's day, with a limited range of radios and radio-cassette players (manufactured by Becker) available as extras. Finding a car with a period radio in working order is a nice bonus, and many companies can now discreetly add USB or Bluetooth connectivity to them. Electric radio aerials (antennas) sometimes jam, but can often be freed with WD40® or a similar product.

Lights

There are few purely electrical problems with these, and the bulbs are easily accessible for quick replacement. On the round style of headlamps fitted to many cars before 1982, the reflectors can suffer corrosion and the trim become bleached. The rubber seals can dry out, letting damp in and causing the lights to steam up. Are the ribbed rear lights – which were specially designed to keep them clean in bad weather – free from cracks?

Check the condition of the headlamp reflectors and trim.

Inspect the rear lights for signs of cracks.

Air-conditioning

Score four points if not fitted: one less thing to cause problems!

Failure of the air-conditioning system to supply cold air is often due to faults with the compressor. On US-market cars fitted with automatic climate control from 1977-81 (recognisable by the horizontal array of buttons on the dashboard), problems can occur with a broken compressor clutch and failed vacuum actuators for the vent controls. The original systems used the now-forbidden R12 refrigerant. They can be updated to use current R134a refrigerants, but this is an expensive job.

If the car steams up when the blower is switched on, this may be due to a blocked drain hole under the windscreen wiper drive spline.

Battery

You will need a multimeter to check the condition of the battery. If in doubt, ask the seller when the battery was last changed, and, if necessary, budget on getting a new one. A trickle charger is also a wise investment, to keep the battery in good condition, especially if you only plan on using the car occasionally.

Engine and mechanicals
Under the bonnet (hood): first impressions

In common with many Mercedes-Benz models of the period, the bonnet can be lifted to a special service position at 90 degrees, which gives great access to the engine. The soundproofing under the bonnet often disintegrates: it looks unsightly, but is easy and relatively inexpensive to replace.

Take a look at the overall condition of the engine bay: are all the belts and hoses – including the polyrib accessory drivebelt – free from cracks or other damage? Can you see any rust, under the battery or at the bottom of the radiator, for instance? The radiators themselves often corrode over time, reducing the circulation of water, and increasing the risk of the engine overheating. If the radiator has been replaced, check that the different hoses and fittings were renewed at the same time. Surface corrosion on the exhaust manifolds, however, is common and not a cause for concern.

280 with bonnet in service position. (Courtesy Mercedes-Benz Classic)

The underbonnet insulation pad on this car has disintegrated, and has been removed altogether until it can be replaced.

Can you see any signs of oil or other fluid leaks? Take a look underneath the car. Minor oil leaks are not uncommon – from the engine, gearbox and rear axle – but the oil consumption should not exceed one litre every 1000km (one US quart per 600 miles). Fuel pipes may corrode and leak, so beware of any smells of fuel around the car.

General mechanical issues   1

The engines fitted to the W123 are incredibly long-lived, with the naturally aspirated diesel engines often reaching over 600,000 miles (one million kilometres) and the petrol units – especially the original M115 four-cylinder engines – covering 300,000 miles (500,000km) without any major work. To perform so well, the engines need frequent oil changes (many owners change the oil every 3000 miles), to avoid sludge building up. New air and fuel filters should also be fitted regularly, and the brake fluid, coolant and sparkplugs changed. Can the seller provide evidence that this regular maintenance has been carried out? Many of these jobs are very simple to carry out at home, and you will find many 'How-To' guides online, through the owners' clubs, for example.

Legions of taxi drivers put their faith in Mercedes' sturdy W123 diesels. (Courtesy Mercedes-Benz Classic)

OM617 five-cylinder diesel on the test bench. (Courtesy Mercedes-Benz Classic)

Scoring: score one of the following three sections (on the usual 4-3-2-1 scale) depending on which engine is fitted to the car you are assessing.

Petrol engines: four-cylinder

The M115 engines fitted to the 200 and 230 until 1980 were already an old design when the W123 was launched, with maximum power developed at a modest 4800rpm, but they have an outstanding reputation for durability. There are a few issues with the Stromberg carburettor fitted, which can result in an uneven idle or rough running when accelerating, but these can normally be resolved without too much difficulty. Uneven running may also point to a leak from the intake manifold, which can be dealt with by replacing the seals. Cars used intensively in city traffic sometimes suffer from problems with the throttle body.

The M102 engines introduced in 1980 in the 200 and 230E were much more modern in design and deliver better performance and fuel economy. They are not, however, considered as durable as the earlier units, and have a notable Achilles heel. The timing chain fitted was of a flawed simplex design and there is a risk that the chain tensioner will fail (particularly in cold weather, when the oil is thick), in turn causing the chain to break. For the W124 series which followed, Mercedes switched to an improved duplex chain design, but on the W123 with the M102 engine, the chain and tensioner should be replaced every 60,000 miles (100,000km). It is essential to check that this work has been done on any car you are considering.

A rattling sound when the engine is under load may be the result of a cracked exhaust manifold: specialists recommend repairing these rather than fitting aftermarket parts, which are likely to be of inferior quality. If the car runs too hot, the thermostat or the magnetic switch for the radiator fan may have failed.

The fuel-injection system fitted to the 230E is generally reliable, but can be complex (and therefore costly) to fix. On cars with carburettors, the mechanical fuel pump can leak. Both M102 units are sensitive to the correct specification of sparkplugs. If the car will not start, but appears to have been well maintained, the fuel pump relay may be at fault: this can be repaired by re-soldering the contacts, or simply be replaced.

Cutaway section of the M102 four-cylinder petrol engine. (Courtesy Mercedes-Benz Classic)

Petrol engines: six-cylinder

The M123 single-cam 2.5-litre 'six' was installed only in the W123 series (in the standard and long-wheelbase saloons and the estate). A refined unit, it was ideally suited to the car. Unfortunately, however, its complex dual down-draft Solex 4A1 carburettor proved extremely difficult to keep in tune, leading to rough running and excessive fuel consumption. Today, there are few specialists who know how to set it up. A good 250 can be very enjoyable, but prospective buyers should go in with their eyes open.

The M123 engine was developed specifically for the W123-series 250. (Courtesy Mercedes-Benz Classic)

Clean-looking 280E engine bay.

The M110 twin-cam 2.8-litre engine is a much more sporting unit, with less torque available under 4000rpm; especially in fuel-injected form (in the 280E, 280CE and 280TE), it is faster and smoother, although somewhat thirstier. An uneven idle may be due to a fault in the fuel-injection, but in general this system is easier to maintain than the carburettors fitted to the 250 and 280. The flexible fuel hoses at the rear of the car tend to degrade over time and will need to be methodically checked and replaced. As on the four-cylinder 230E, the fuel pump relay can fail.

When assessing a 280E, it is essential to ensure that the engine is in good condition, as its twin-cam design, with an all-alloy head, makes major work much more expensive. An all-new engine costs ●x6000! Ensure that the cooling system has been regularly maintained, and watch for failed head gaskets and cracks in the cylinder block. High oil consumption and blue smoke from the exhaust can denote worn piston rings.

Diesel engines: four- and five-cylinder

The diesel engines in the W123 are among the toughest car engines ever made. They require no electrics or electronics to run, apart from the glow plugs to start them, so there is precious little which can go wrong. The five-cylinder turbodiesel unit is slightly more complex, but delivers much better performance. That robustness can, however, lead some owners to cut corners, and some cars have even been run on waste vegetable oil!

It is important therefore to verify that the engine oil and filter have been changed on a regular basis. The valve clearances need to be checked every 15,000 miles: if they get out of adjustment, the car may be reluctant to start or will run unevenly. The timing chain should be inspected at the same time. Most other issues, such as failed head gaskets, faulty glow plugs or fuel injectors (which can cause increased fuel consumption), can be fixed quite easily. At very high mileages, the vacuum pump may fail, but replacements are available. On the five-cylinder (OM617) engines, excessive vibration may be due to a defective flywheel.

The five-cylinder OM617 was Mercedes' first turbocharged diesel engine to enter production. (Courtesy Mercedes-Benz Classic)

Exhaust system

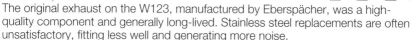

The original exhaust on the W123, manufactured by Eberspächer, was a high-quality component and generally long-lived. Stainless steel replacements are often unsatisfactory, fitting less well and generating more noise.

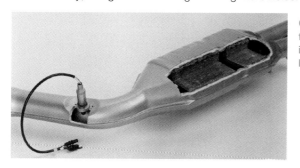

Catalytic converter from a late-model W123 in 1984. (Courtesy Mercedes-Benz Classic)

Transmission

Scoring: score one of the following two sections (on the usual 4-3-2-1 scale) depending on whether the car you are assessing is fitted with manual or automatic transmission.

Manual transmission

With proper maintenance – the gearbox oil should be changed every 36,000 miles (60,000km) – the manual transmission on the W123 should give good service over several hundred thousand miles. Most manual gearboxes on the diesels and four-cylinder petrols were four-speed units, with the five-speed transmission most commonly found on the sporty 280E models. Even when new, the gearchange was somewhat notchy, but watch for weak synchromesh when changing into second gear. The shaft bearings can also wear: if you hear any bearing noise, this should be addressed at once to avoid further damage. A screeching sound suggests that the differential may be on its way out. Like all rubber components, the driveshaft gaiters can perish with age, letting in dirt.

Automatic transmission

The four-speed automatic transmissions fitted to many W123s are also robust and usually reliable. Provided that the oil is changed regularly, they should cover 200,000 miles (320,000km) or more, without major work. It is worth changing the oil cooler pipes for the transmission under the radiator on a preventive basis, especially if the radiator has to be removed.

When testing the car, watch for juddering when taking up drive (forwards or in reverse), and for the engine revs flaring during gearchanges. In either case, a professional overhaul of the transmission will be needed, or it may be cheaper to fit a good,

With the automatic transmission, check that all four forward speeds and reverse operate smoothly.

secondhand unit. There are relatively few mechanics with experience of working on Mercedes' automatic transmissions of this generation.

Suspension ④ ③ ② ①

The suspension on the W123 was an advanced design when the model was introduced. The weight of the car can cause wear to the bushings, springs and shock absorbers, but it is a conventional set-up which requires few special checks. To make sure that the shock absorbers still work properly, lean heavily on one corner of the car and let go: the car should bounce back once and then settle. The springs can suffer from cracks, which can sometimes be hard to spot, but corrosion on other suspension components such as the lower spring mounts, front anti-roll bar and rear

The front assembly of the W123 laid bare. (Courtesy Mercedes-Benz Classic)

trailing arms can be easier to see with the car on a lift. Wear in the front lower ball joints can cause uneven tyre wear: the joints are not expensive to replace, but require a press to fix them in place. If the rear wheel bearings play up, these need a special tool to replace them.

The estates and long-wheelbase saloons were fitted, as standard, with hydraulic self-levelling rear suspension to cope with the extra payload they could carry. You can test that this is operating correctly by loading the rear of the car, or have two people sit on the tailgate opening with the engine running. If the tail of the car sags, it may be nothing more than a sticking height control lever inside the car, which some lubricant should easily free up. A full overhaul, however, will include checking the regulator valve and the pump, and for signs of leaks from the seals; the pressure accumulator may also have lost gas. When the system is completely dry, the ride will become abnormally firm.

Steering ④ ③ ② ①

The W123 remained faithful to Mercedes' traditional recirculating ball-type steering. A small amount of play around the straight-ahead position is normal, but if it is excessive, the car will fail a safety inspection such as the MoT test in the UK. Some adjustment of the steering box is possible, but an expensive replacement (●x2000) may be the only solution. A tendency to drift in high winds can often be cured by replacing the steering damper, which is much more affordable.

Large-diameter steering wheel typical of Mercedes of the period: check for excess play.

Tyres

Look for cracks and suspicious bulges in the sidewalls. All the tyres (including the spare) should be of the same type, from a good-quality brand and manufactured recently (see Chapter 15 for guidance on reading the DOT code). Make sure that the correct tyres are fitted according to the model: most of the saloons came with SR-rated 175-section tyres, but the coupés, estates and 280/280E saloons all had wider 195-section tyres with an HR rating, to cope with their increased weight and/or performance. The long-wheelbase saloons had 185 HR tyres mounted on 15in wheels, rather than the 14in wheels shared by the other versions.

Don't forget to check the condition of the spare tyre and wheel under the boot floor.

The correct tyre pressures can be found on this sticker inside the fuel filler cover.

Brakes

All W123 models are fitted with fully hydraulically operated disc brakes all round and cable-operated rear handbrake shoes inside specially designed drums. The estates are fitted with the bigger rear discs from the W116 S-Class. Other than an annual change of brake fluid, the system requires little maintenance. Its main weakness concerns the master cylinder: the seals on this can disintegrate, causing the brakes to stick. Some owners therefore replace the master cylinder on a preventive basis. Other than this, the brake lines can rust, while the flexible hoses can perish, or close up inside, so restricting the flow of brake fluid and impairing the efficiency of the brakes.

Right-hand drive cars have a pull-out parking brake at the end of the dashboard.

Vacuum system ④ ③ ② ①

Mercedes used a vacuum system for the centralised door locking, air-conditioning system, and, until 1984, the vacuum modulators of the automatic transmission. If the doors do not unlock properly, there may be a problem with the vacuum pump – which is not too expensive to replace – or a leak in the system, which can be laborious to track down.

Make sure that the vacuum-operated central locking system works correctly.

Underbody ④ ③ ② ①

A thick layer of underseal can be a sign of a caring owner ... or hide a multitude of sins! A small screwdriver can help you gently probe any suspicious areas. Cars originally sold in South Africa, on the other hand, had no underbody wax protection at all. If you can look at the car on a lift or from an inspection pit, take the chance to look for corrosion on the chassis members, rear subframe and suspension components, and inspect the exhaust system, brake and fuel lines. On the estate, the fuel tank was of a special shape: if it is dented, it will not allow the fuel to flow correctly.

Professional inspection

Having your car inspected by a Mercedes specialist can often be a sound investment, giving you extra peace of mind when buying a good car ... and maybe saving you from buying a 'bad 'un.' No genuine seller should object to this, provided of course that you cover any costs involved.

A professional inspection in a workshop will give you the chance to look at the car on a hoist, and to carry out some additional checks, such as the valve clearances and cylinder compressions, which require specialist equipment. On cars with little service history or especially high mileages, these tests may give you added peace of mind.

Evaluation procedure

Add up the total points from each section.

Score: 124 (coupé or estate)/116 (saloon) = perfect; 93/87 = good; 62/58 = average; 31/29 = buyer beware! Cars scoring over 93/87 should be completely usable and require the minimum of repair or rectification, although continued service maintenance and care will be required to keep them in good condition. Cars scoring between 62/58 and 92/86 will require serious work (at much the same cost regardless of score). Cars scoring between 31/29 and 61/57 will require very careful assessment of the repair costs needed.

www.velocebooks.com / www.veloce.co.uk
Details of all current books • New book news • Special offers • Gift vouchers • Forum

43

10 Auctions
– sold! Another way to buy your dream

Auction pros & cons

Pros: Prices are often lower than those of dealers or private sellers, and you might grab a real bargain on the day. Auctioneers have usually established clear title with the seller. At the venue, you can usually examine documentation relating to the vehicle.

Cons: You have to rely on a sketchy catalogue description of condition and history. The opportunity to inspect is limited, and you cannot drive the car. Auction cars are often a little below par and may require some work. It's easy to overbid. There will usually be a buyer's premium to pay in addition to the auction hammer price.

Which auction?

Auctions by established auctioneers are advertised in car magazines and on the auction houses' websites. A catalogue, or a simple printed list of the lots for auctions might only be available a day or two ahead, though often lots are listed and pictured on auctioneers' websites much earlier. Contact the auction company to ask if previous auction selling prices are available as this is useful information (details of past sales are often available on websites).

Catalogue, entry fee, and payment details

When you purchase the catalogue of vehicles in an auction, it often acts as a ticket allowing two people to attend the viewing days and the auction. Catalogue details tend to be comparatively brief, but will include information such as 'one owner from new, low mileage, full service history,' etc. It will also usually show a guide price to give you some idea of what to expect to pay and will tell you what is charged as a 'Buyer's premium.' The catalogue will also contain details of acceptable forms of payment. At the fall of the hammer, an immediate deposit is usually required, the balance payable within 24 hours. If the plan is to pay by cash, there may be a cash limit. Some auctions will accept payment by debit card. Sometimes credit or charge cards are acceptable, but will often incur an extra charge. A bank draft or bank transfer will have to be arranged in advance with your own bank, as well as with the auction house. No car will be released before all payments are cleared. If delays occur in payment transfers, then storage costs can accrue.

Buyer's premium

A buyer's premium will be added to the hammer price: don't forget this in your calculations. It is not usual for there to be a further state tax or local tax on the purchase price and/or on the buyer's premium.

Viewing

In some instances, it's possible to view on the day, or days before, as well as in the hours prior to, the auction. There are auction officials available who are willing to help out by opening engine and luggage compartments, and to allow you to inspect the interior. While the officials may start the engine for you, a test drive is out of the question. Crawling under and around the car as much as you want is permitted, but you can't suggest that the car you are interested in be jacked up, or attempt to do the job yourself. You can also ask to see any documentation available.

Bidding

Before you take part in the auction, decide your maximum bid – and stick to it!

It may take a while for the auctioneer to reach the lot you are interested in, so use that time to observe how other bidders behave. When it's the turn of your car, attract the auctioneer's attention and make an early bid. The auctioneer will then look to you for a reaction every time another bid is made; usually the bids will be in fixed increments until the bidding slows, when smaller increments will often be accepted before the hammer falls. If you want to withdraw from the bidding, make sure the auctioneer understands your intentions – a vigorous shake of the head when he or she looks to you for the next bid should do the trick!

Assuming that you are the successful bidder, the auctioneer will note your card or paddle number, and, from that moment on, you will be responsible for the vehicle.

If the car is unsold, either because it failed to reach the reserve or because there was little interest, it may be possible to negotiate with the owner, via the auctioneers, after the sale is over.

Successful bid

There are two more items to think about. How to get the car home, and insurance. If you can't drive the car, your own or a hired trailer is one way; another is to have the vehicle shipped using the facilities of a local company. The auction house will also have details of companies specialising in the transfer of cars.

Insurance for immediate cover can usually be purchased on site, but it may be more cost-effective to make arrangements with your own insurance company in advance, and then call to confirm the full details.

eBay and other online auctions

eBay and other online auctions could land you a car at a bargain price, though you'd be foolhardy to bid without examining the car first, something most vendors encourage. A useful feature of eBay is that the geographical location of the car is shown, so you can narrow your choices to those within a realistic radius of home. Be prepared to be outbid in the last few moments of the auction. Remember, your bid is binding and that it will be very, very difficult to get restitution in the case of a crooked vendor fleecing you – *caveat emptor!*

Be aware that some cars offered for sale in online auctions are 'ghost' cars. Don't part with any cash without being sure that the vehicle actually exists and is as described (usually pre-bidding inspection is possible).

Auctioneers

Barrett-Jackson www.barrett-jackson.com/ **Bonhams** www.bonhams.com/ **British Car Auctions BCA)** www.bca-europe.com or www.british-car-auctions. co.uk/ **Christies** www.christies.com/ **Coys** www.coys.co.uk/ **eBay** www.eBay. com/ **H&H** www.handh.co.uk/ **RM Sotheby's** www.rmsothebys.com/ **Shannons** www.shannons.com.au/ **Silver** www.silverauctions.com

11 Paperwork
– correct documentation is essential!

The paper trail
Enthusiasts' cars often come with a large portfolio of paperwork accumulated by a succession of proud owners. This documentation represents the real history of the car and shows the level of care the car has received, how it's been used, which specialists have worked on it and the dates of major repairs.

Registration documents
All countries/states have some form of registration for private vehicles, whether it's like the American 'pink slip' system or the British 'log book' system.

It is essential to check that the registration document is genuine, that it relates to the car in question, and that all the vehicle's details are correctly recorded, including chassis/VIN and engine numbers (if these are shown). If you are buying from the previous owner, his or her name and address will be recorded in the document; this will not be the case if you are buying from a dealer.

In the UK, the current registration document is named 'V5C,' and is printed in coloured sections of blue, green and pink. The blue section relates to the car specification, the green section has details of the new owner, and the pink section is sent to the DVLA in the UK when the car is sold. A small section in yellow deals with selling the car within the motor trade.

In the UK, the DVLA will provide details of earlier keepers of the vehicle upon payment of a small fee, and much can be learned in this way.

If the car has a foreign registration, there may be expensive and time-consuming formalities to complete. Do you really want the hassle?

Roadworthiness certificate
Most country/state administrations require that vehicles are regularly tested to prove that they are safe to use on the public highway and do not produce excessive emissions. In the UK, that test (the 'MoT') is carried out at approved testing stations, for a fee. In the US, the requirement varies, but most states insist on an emissions test every two years as a minimum, while the police are charged with pulling over unsafe-looking vehicles.

In the UK, the test is required on an annual basis, once a vehicle becomes three years old. Of particular relevance for older cars is that the certificate issued includes the mileage reading recorded at the test date, and, therefore, becomes an independent record of that car's history. Ask the seller if previous certificates are available. Without an MoT, the vehicle should be trailered to its new home, unless you insist that a valid MoT is part of the deal. (Not such a bad idea this, as at least you will know the car was roadworthy on the day it was tested, and you don't need to wait for the old certificate to expire before having the test done.)

Road licence
The administration of nearly every country/state charges some kind of tax for the use of its road system, the actual form of the 'road licence' and, how it is displayed, varying enormously country to country and state to state.

Whatever form of 'road licence,' it must relate to the vehicle carrying it and must be present and valid, if the car is to be driven on the public highway legally. The value of the licence will depend on the length of time it will continue to be valid.

Changed legislation in the UK means that the seller of a car must surrender any existing road fund licence, and it is the responsibility of the new owner to re-tax the vehicle at the time of purchase and before the car can be driven on the road. It's therefore vital to see the Vehicle Registration Certificate (V5C) at the time of purchase, and to have access to the New Keeper Supplement (V5C/2), allowing the buyer to obtain road tax immediately.

If the car is untaxed because it has not been used for a period of time, the owner has to inform the licensing authorities, otherwise the vehicle's date-related registration number will be lost and there will be a painful amount of paperwork to get it re-registered.

Valuation certificate

A private vendor may have a recent valuation certificate, or letter signed by a recognised expert stating how much he, or she, believes the particular car to be worth (such documents, together with photos, are usually needed to get 'agreed value' insurance). Generally, such documents should act only as confirmation of your own assessment of the car rather than a guarantee of value. The easiest way to find out how to obtain a formal valuation is to contact the owners' club.

VIN and option data

Each Mercedes left the factory with a detailed data card, describing the exact model, colour and trim, and the codes for each option fitted. This information is also stamped on a metal data plate at the front of the engine bay or, for cars delivered new to the US, on the door pillar. These codes – which you can look up on many online sites – should correspond to the actual equipment on the car you are viewing, and provide valuable confirmation of its authenticity. If the card is missing, Mercedes-Benz' Classic department in your country may be able to supply a replacement.

Stamped option plate under the bonnet of a UK-market W123.

VIN plate for a right-hand drive automatic 250.

The 17-digit VIN (Vehicle Identification Number) on the data card should tally with that on the car, which you can again find inside the driver's door jamb or in the engine compartment. It may also be etched on the windows as a security measure.

Service history

Try to obtain as much service history and other paperwork pertaining to the car as you can. Naturally, dealer stamps, or specialist garage receipts score most points in the value stakes. However, anything helps in the great authenticity game, items such as the original bill of sale, handbook, parts invoices and repair bills adding to the story and the character of the car. Even a brochure correct to the year of the car's manufacture is a useful document and something that you could well have to search hard to locate in future years. If the seller claims that the car has been restored, then expect receipts and other evidence from a specialist restorer.

If the seller claims to have carried out regular servicing at home, ask what work was completed, when, and seek some evidence of it being carried out. Your assessment of the car's overall condition should tell you whether the seller's claims are genuine.

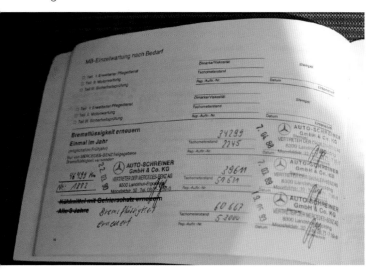

If available, the service booklet will provide valuable information on the car's history.

Restoration photographs

If the seller tells you that the car has undergone significant work, ask to be shown a series of photographs taken while the work was underway. These should help you gauge the thoroughness of the work. If you buy the car, ask if you can have all the photographs, as they form an important part of the vehicle's history. It's surprising how many sellers are happy to part with their car and accept your cash, but want to hang on to their photographs! In the latter event, you may be able to persuade the vendor to get a set of copies made.

Previous ownership records

Due to the introduction of important new legislation on data protection, it is no longer possible to acquire, from the British DVLA, a list of previous owners of a car you own, or are intending to purchase. This scenario will also apply to dealerships, and other specialists, whom you may wish to contact to acquire information on previous ownership and work carried out.

12 What's it worth?
– let your head rule your heart

Condition

If the car you've been looking at is really bad, then you've probably not bothered to use the marking system in Chapter 9 – 60-minute evaluation. You may not have even got as far as using that chapter at all!

If you did use the marking system in Chapter 9, you'll know whether the car is in Excellent (maybe Concours), Good, Average or Poor condition or, perhaps, somewhere in-between these categories.

Many enthusiasts' car magazines run a regular price guide. If you haven't bought the latest editions, do so now, and compare their suggested values for the model you are thinking of buying; also look at the auction prices they're reporting. The values published in the magazines tend to vary from one magazine to another, as do their scales of condition, so read carefully the guidance notes they provide. Bear in mind that a car that is truly a recent show winner could be worth more than the highest scale published. Assuming that the car you have in mind is not in show/concours condition, then relate the level of condition that you judge the car to be in with the appropriate guide price. How does the figure compare with the asking price? Before you start haggling with the seller, consider what effect any variation from standard specification might have on the car's value. If you are buying from a dealer, remember there will be a dealer's premium on the price.

Sunroof: a popular extra on all models. (Courtesy Mercedes-Benz Classic)

Automatic transmission, unmarked leather upholstery and period radio in this 250.

Prices of the W123 coupés and estates (wagons) have already moved up considerably, with a knock-on effect on saloons (sedans) in good condition. Buying a cheap car (under ●x4000) can prove a false economy, if it needs replacement tyres, rubber seals, or expensive chrome trim.

Desirable options/extras

When it was launched, the W123 had little in the way of standard equipment: power-assisted steering, electric windows, head restraints and rear seatbelts were all extra on most models, and there was a lengthy options list. Some options are quite rare: heated front seats, a driver's airbag and – in Europe especially – air-conditioning, for example. With a car of this age, it is better to concentrate on finding a vehicle in really good condition rather than

holding out for an unusual extra. Some more common options, however, are worth looking for.

Power steering is always desirable, making the car far more pleasant to drive. Many buyers prefer Mercedes' smooth-shifting automatic transmission. A sliding sunroof can be a good substitute for air-conditioning, while tinted glass can protect the interior trim from cracks and fading. Inside the car, leather upholstery – which can be identified by the six, or more, narrower pleated sections in the seats – looks classy, but for durability, nothing can beat Mercedes' legendary MB-Tex (vinyl) upholstery (which has five broader, pleated sections). The luxurious velour upholstery is rare, except on coupés.

Many enthusiasts love Mercedes' traditional painted hubcaps, but the optional Fuchs alloy wheels are particularly sought-after on the coupé. On the estate, the folding third row of seats in the luggage compartment is especially desirable.

Undesirable features

Some owners prefer the most basic 'poverty spec' models for their sheer simplicity, but unassisted manual steering certainly detracts from the cars' appeal on the road. Period colours like Apricot or Mimosa are very much an acquired taste, and may make the car harder to sell on later. And, if you choose a diesel saloon (sedan) finished in Light Ivory, be ready for countless 'Frankfurt taxi' jokes!

In period, many companies – including AMG, Brabus, Lorinser and Zender – sold alloy wheels, bodykits and special interior trim for the W123. The quality of some of the cheaper parts was poor and can detract from the cars' classic appearance. Today, most buyers prefer unmodified, original cars.

Striking a deal

Negotiate on the basis of your condition assessment, mileage, and fault rectification cost. Also take into account the car's specification. Be realistic about the value, but don't be completely intractable: a small compromise on the part of the vendor or buyer will often facilitate a deal at little real cost.

Beware of cars without power steering. (Courtesy Mercedes-Benz Classic)

13 Do you really want to restore?
– it'll take longer and cost more than you think

The W123 is probably too tough a car for its own good. After racking up many miles early in its life in Western Europe, North America and across the globe, many of the cars have gone on to second, and third, lives as taxis and workhorses in Eastern Europe or North Africa. Often, they carry huge loads and are run with minimal maintenance.

Desperate to find estate (wagon) models in particular, some collectors have even purchased cars in countries like Morocco to rebuild completely. For enthusiasts like these, the satisfaction of deciding exactly which parts to replace and doing the work themselves cannot be matched. Other collectors may lack the skills or facilities to restore a car themselves, but will seek perfection, at almost any price. Some leading W123 specialists such as W123 World, run by Mark Cosovich in South Wales (UK), can restore a W123 to a customer's specification and 'as new' condition, complete with a 12-month warranty.

For the majority of would-be W123 owners, however, it is hard to justify the cost of a full-scale restoration. Trim parts, body panels and major mechanical components do not come cheap, before taking into account labour costs for any work which has to be undertaken by a professional workshop or specialist. If the recent increases in the prices of top-quality estates and coupés continue, it is possible that rebuilding models such as a 280TE estate or 280CE coupé will make economic sense. At present, however, it is unlikely that the cost of a high-quality restoration will be recouped.

For the moment therefore, each case needs to be looked at very carefully, to determine exactly what work is required and how much it will cost. Some interesting 'barn find' cars, such as an unusual manual 280E with low mileage, may turn out to be in better shape than they first appear, but such cases are rare. Entry-level cars, such as a 200 saloon with few extras, may be simpler to restore, but their market value, once restored, will be lower, too.

If you are looking at a car which has already been restored, find out as much as you can about the work: when was it carried out, and by whom? Ideally, the work will have been done by a recognised Mercedes-Benz specialist, using OEM or the best available replacement parts, and fitted using the right specialist tools. Be wary of older restorations, which may not have been carried out to the same standard as a rebuild today. Many restorers keep a detailed photographic record of the jobs they have done, and these can be invaluable in assessing the quality of the restoration work.

A stripped-down saloon bodyshell, seen at the Retro Classics show in Stuttgart.

14 Paint problems

– bad complexion, including dimples, pimples and bubbles

When new, the W123 received seven coats of primer and paint to ensure a high-quality finish.

Paint faults generally occur due to lack of protection/maintenance, or to poor preparation prior to a respray or touch-up. Some of the following conditions may be present in the car you're looking at:

Orange peel

This appears as an uneven paint surface, similar to the skin of an orange. This fault is caused by the failure of atomized paint droplets to flow into each other when they hit the surface. It is sometimes possible to rub out the effect with proprietary paint cutting/rubbing compound or very fine grades of abrasive paper. A respray may be necessary in severe cases. Consult a bodywork repairer/paint shop for advice on the particular car.

Cracking

Severe cases are likely to have been caused by too heavy an application of paint (or filler beneath the paint). Also, insufficient stirring of the paint before application can lead to the components being improperly mixed, and cracking can result. Incompatibility with the paint already on the panel can have a similar effect. To rectify the problem, it is necessary to rub down to a smooth, sound finish before respraying the problem area.

Crazing

Sometimes the paint takes on a crazed, rather than a cracked, appearance when the problems mentioned under 'Cracking' are present. This problem can also be caused by a reaction between the underlying surface and the paint. Paint removal and respraying the problem area is usually the only solution.

Rust bubbling away under the paint on the tailgate of this estate (wagon).

Blistering

Almost always caused by corrosion of the metal beneath the paint. Usually perforation will be found in the metal and the damage will usually be worse than that suggested by the area of blistering. The metal will have to be repaired before repainting.

Micro blistering

Usually the result of an economy respray, where inadequate heating has allowed moisture to settle on the car before spraying. Consult a paint specialist, but usually damaged paint will have to be removed before partial or full respraying. Can also be caused by car covers that don't 'breathe.'

52

Fading

Some colours, especially reds, are prone to fading, if subjected to strong sunlight for long periods without the benefit of polish protection. Sometimes proprietary paint restorers and/or paint cutting/rubbing compounds will retrieve the situation. Often a respray is the only real solution.

Peeling

Often a problem with metallic paintwork when the sealing lacquer becomes damaged and begins to peel off. The earliest W123s with metallic paint finishes did not have a clear lacquer coat, leaving the paint itself exposed. Poorly applied paint may also peel. The remedy is to strip and start again!

Dimples

Dimples in the paintwork are caused by the residue of polish (particularly silicone types) not being removed properly before respraying. Paint removal and repainting is the only solution.

Dents

Small dents are usually easily cured by the 'Dentmaster' or equivalent process, that sucks or pushes out the dent (as long as the paint surface is still intact). Companies offering dent removal services usually come to your home: consult your telephone directory or search online.

Bold colours such as this yellow are very much of their time.

15 Problems due to lack of use

– just like their owners, W123s need exercise!

There is no need to fear high mileage on any of the W123 models, and lack of use can bring a different set of problems, so take particular care if you are looking at a car which has been laid up for some time.

Seized and rusted components

Pistons in callipers, slave and master cylinders can seize. The parking brake can seize if the cables and linkages rust, particularly on cars with automatic transmission, where some owners simply put the transmission selector in 'P' and do not use the parking brake at all.

Fluids

All fluids should be replaced at regular intervals, and, if filled, the air-conditioning recharged. Good-quality coolant is essential to avoid premature corrosion in the engine, cooling and heating system, and to avoid the risk of serious damage. Silt settling and solidifying can result in overheating.

Brake fluid absorbs water from the atmosphere, and should be renewed every year on the W123.

Fuel system

On the K-Jetronic system fitted to cars with fuel-injection, the mixture control can play up if the car is not used for a long time. Rust damage to the fuel tank can be especially costly to put right, as rust particles from the tank can get into the fuel system. In the worst cases, the entire fuel system, including the filter and fuel pump, may need to be replaced.

Rotting exhaust system

Exhaust gas contains a high water content, so exhaust systems corrode very quickly from the inside when the car is not used. This even applies to stainless steel systems.

Tyre problems

Tyres that have had the weight of the car on them in a single position for some time will develop flat spots, resulting in some (usually temporary) vibration. The tyre walls may have cracks or (blister-type) bulges, meaning new tyres are needed. Even if the tyres appear to be in good condition, check the DOT code on the sidewall, which will show you the week and year of manufacture.

This tyre is from week 13 of 2015, as shown by the '1315' DOT code.

Shock absorbers (dampers)
With lack of use, the dampers will lose their elasticity or even seize. Creaking, groaning and stiff suspension are signs of this problem.

Rubber and plastic
Radiator hoses may have perished and split, possibly resulting in the loss of all coolant. Window, door and rear light seals can all harden and leak. Gaiters and boots can crack. Wiper blades will harden.

The underbonnet insulation pad will perish, even when the car is unused.

Interior trim
On cars fitted with leather upholstery, the hide needs regular conditioning (every six months) if it is to stay supple and in good condition. Cars left in the sun can suffer from dried or cracked dashboards and other trim. Velour or cloth trim can fade, especially in exposed areas like the top of the rear seat on saloons (sedans) and coupés.

Electrics
The battery will be of little use if it has not been charged for many months. If a car is left standing for several weeks, connecting it to a trickle charger will keep it in good condition.

Earthing/grounding problems are common when the connections have corroded. Wiring insulation can harden and fail.

www.velocebooks.com / www.veloce.co.uk
Details of all current books • New book news • Special offers • Gift vouchers • Forum

55

16 The community
– key people, organisations and companies in the W123 world

The W123 series is now well established as a classic Mercedes, and owners will find plenty of help to look after their cars from a wide network of clubs and independent specialists, as well as Mercedes-Benz itself.

Clubs

Mercedes-Benz lends its support to more than 80 independent clubs worldwide, and many of these have sections or model registers dedicated to the W123. Benefits available to members include technical helplines and other information, discounted services such as insurance, professionally produced club magazines, and the chance to join frequent social and driving events. You can find out more at:

• Mercedes-Benz Classic (factory homepage):
mercedes-benz.com/en/mercedes-benz/classic/classic-overview/
• UK: mercedes-benz-club.co.uk
• North America: mbca.org
• Other countries: specials.mercedes-benz-classic.com/en/club/#ger

Specialists

In North America, it's worth starting with one of the 85 local sections of the club, which should be able to recommend a dealer or workshop near you.

In the UK, independent specialists such as these should be able to look after your car, and some of them also sell W123s:

• Roger Edwards Motors (Buckinghamshire): see Facebook page
or call 01494 766766
• John Haynes Mercedes (West Sussex): john-haynes.com
• Martyn Marrocco Classic Cars (North Yorkshire): see Facebook page
or call 01653 692309
• Steve Redfearn Motor Co (London): call 020 8540 2311
• ToWiW123 (Sheffield): theonlywayisw123.wixsite.com/towiw123/
• W123 World (Swansea): w123world.com/

You will find listings for many other companies in the club directories and in the magazines below.

Parts and accessories

Many service parts remain available from your local Mercedes-Benz dealer, with support from the factory in Germany or the Mercedes-Benz Classic Center in Irvine, California. Their prices can sometimes be high, so you may prefer to order online from an independent parts supplier such as these:

• UK – Mercedes Parts Centre: mercedes-parts-centre.co.uk
and PFS Parts: partsformercedes-benz.com
• US – Pelican Parts: pelicanparts.com/catalog/

Useful sources of information

Three English-language magazines cater to classic Mercedes enthusiasts, and often feature the W123:

- *Mercedes Enthusiast* (monthly – mercedesenthusiast.co.uk) and *Classic Mercedes* (quarterly – classicmercedesmagazine.com) can be found at large newsstands in both the UK and North America, or obtained on subscription
- *Mercedes-Benz Classic* is published in English and German by Mercedes itself three times a year: subscribe at mercedes-benz.com/en/mercedes-benz/lifestyle/mercedes-benz-magazines/classic-magazine/subscription/
- In addition to Mercedes' own manuals and technical literature, two books covering the history of the W123 can be recommended: *Mercedes-Benz W123 series 1976-1986* by long-term marque enthusiast Brian Long from Veloce Publishing (veloce.co.uk), and *Mercedes-Benz W123 – The finest saloon car of the 20th Century?* by Martin Buckley and Mark Cosovich (w123world.com). Brooklands Books (brooklandsbooks.co.uk) and Bentley Publishers (bentleypublishers.com) both publish an Owners' Workshop Manual for the series.

For enthusiasts who want to carry out repair work themselves, Kent Bergsma's informative Mercedessource channel on YouTube features more than 80 'How-To' videos on the W123. In the UK, the official club (mercedes-benz-club.co.uk) has archived a large number of very helpful features from its magazine, covering common problems and how to repair them. Even if you do not plan on doing the work yourself, these resources provide valuable guidance on how difficult (and potentially expensive) a job may be.

W123 saloon on show at the entrance to the Mercedes-Benz Museum in Stuttgart.
(Courtesy Mercedes-Benz Classic)

17 Vital statistics
– essential data at your fingertips

Production figures

Body style	Number built
Saloons (sedans): standard-wheelbase	2,375,440
Saloons (sedans): long-wheelbase	13,700
Coupés	99,884
Estates (wagons)	199,517
Chassis only (for special bodies)	8373
Total	**2,696,914**

About 40% of all cars built were exported, and more than half (54%) were fitted with diesel engines.

Technical specifications
Engine and transmission: petrol models

Model	Production period	Engine capacity (cc)	Engine type	Configuration	Peak power (bhp) at rpm	Maximum torque (lb/ft) at rpm	Transmissions available
200	1976-80	1988	M115	4-cyl in-line	94/4800	117/3000	4M/4A
200	1980-85	1997	M102	4-cyl in-line	109/5200	125/3000	4M or 5M/4A
230	1976-80	2307	M115	4-cyl in-line	109/4800	137/3000	4M/4A
230E	1980-85	2299	M102	4-cyl in-line	136/5100	151/3500	4M or 5M/4A
250	1976-85	2525	M123	6-cyl in-line	129/5500*	145/3500*	4M or 5M/4A
280E	1975-85	2746	M110	6-cyl in-line	177/6000†	173/4500†	4M or 5M/4A

* Increased to 140bhp at 5500rpm and 148lb/ft at 3500rpm from September 1979.
† Increased to 185bhp at 5800 rpm and 177lb/ft on European 280E models from April 1978.

Engine and transmission: diesel models

Model	Production period	Engine capacity (cc)	Engine type	Cylinders & layout	Peak power (bhp) at rpm	Maximum torque (lb/ft) at rpm	Transmissions available
200D	1976-85	1988	OM615	4-cyl in-line	55/4200*	83/2400	4M or 5M/4A†
220D	1976-79	2197	OM615	4-cyl in-line	60/4200	93/2400	4M/4A
240D	1976-85	2404‡	OM616	4-cyl in-line	65/4200‡	101/2400	4M or 5M/4A†
300D	1976-85	3005§	OM617	5-cyl in-line	80/4000§	127/2400	4M or 5M/4A†

300D Turbo-diesel	1981-85	2998	OM617	5-cyl in-line	121/4350¶	170/2400¶	4A

* Increased to 60bhp at 4400rpm in February 1979.
† Five-speed manual optional from February 1982.
‡ Engine revised in August 1978, to give 2399cc displacement. Power increased to 72bhp at 4400rpm.
§ Engine revised in August 1978, to give 2998cc displacement. Power increased to 88bhp at 4400rpm.
¶ Increased to 125bhp at 4350rpm and 184lb/ft at 2400rpm in October 1982.

Running gear
Independent suspension all round. Self-levelling rear suspension on estates and long-wheelbase saloons.
Steering by recirculating ball, with power assistance available as an option or standard, depending on model.
Four-wheel disc brakes, with optional ABS from October 1980.
14in wheels on all models except long-wheelbase saloons (15in).

Performance figures: selected models

Model	Top speed	Acceleration: 0-100kph (62mph) in seconds
200 manual (M115 engine)	99mph (160kph)	15.2
230CE automatic	109mph (175kph)	12.3
280TE automatic	121mph (195kph)	11.2
200D manual (55bhp)	81mph (130kph)	31.0
240D manual (72bhp)	89mph (143kph)	22.0
300D automatic (88bhp)	93mph (150kph)	19.2
300TD Turbodiesel automatic	103mph (165kph)	15.0

Source: *Young Classics: Mercedes-Benz W123* (Delius Klasing Verlag).

Dimensions

Model	Length	Width	Height	Wheelbase	Fuel tank
Saloon (sedan)	186.0in/ 4725mm	70.3in/ 1786mm	56.6in/ 1438mm	110.0in/ 2795mm	65l (17.2US gal)/80l (21.1US gal) on 6-cyl models
Coupé	182.7in/ 4640mm	70.3in/ 1786mm	54.9in/ 1395mm	106.7in/ 2710mm	65l (17.2US gal)/80l (21.1US gal) on 6-cyl models
Estate (wagon)	186.0in/ 4725mm	70.3in/ 1786mm	57.9in/ 1470mm	110.0in/ 2795mm	70l (18.5US gal)
LWB saloon	210.8in/ 5355mm	70.3in/ 1786mm	58.3in/ 1480mm	134.8in/ 3425mm	65l (17.2US gal)

Weight
1340kg-1630kg (2950-3600lb), depending on model and equipment.

The Essential Buyer's Guide™ series ...